SLEEP TIME

T0053810

Sleep Time, part of the 'Words Together' series, has been created to support children to understand and use two-word sentences.

Using the pivot word 'sleeping', the simple story and repetitious structure provide an opportunity for the child to hear and experience the sentence structure in new ways. Bright and colourful illustrations provide rich opportunities for conversation and engagement.

This storybook is an exciting resource for early years practitioners, parents, and those working with children at an early stage of speech and language development.

Kate Freeman is a highly experienced speech and language therapist, consultant and former charity director. She is also a mum to three grown-up sons, and a grandmother. Kate's passion is working with children and families, making a difference to their futures.

Kate's career has included working with children, families, groups, local authorities, charities and commercial organisations, providing an insight into the skills of communication and how children learn to talk.

Jenny Edge is a professional artist and illustrator working in a wide range of mediums and styles. She enjoys producing colourful, decorative and ornamental paintings as well as the figurative work she trained in at art school. Although based in Warwickshire, her work can be found all over the world in both domestic and commercial interiors.

SLEEP TIME

A 'WORDS TOGETHER' STORYBOOK TO HELP CHILDREN FIND THEIR VOICES

Kate Freeman
Illustrated by Jenny Edge

Routledge
Taylor & Francis Group

LONDON AND NEW YORK

Cover image: © Jenny Edge

First published 2022

by Routledge

2 Park Square, Milton Park, Abingdon, Oxon OX14 4RN

and by Routledge

605 Third Avenue, New York, NY 10158

Routledge is an imprint of the Taylor & Francis Group, an informa business

© 2022 Kate Freeman and Jenny Edge

The right of Kate Freeman to be identified as author of this work and Jenny Edge to be identified as illustrator of this work has been asserted in accordance with sections 77 and 78 of the Copyright, Designs and Patents Act 1988.

All rights reserved. No part of this book may be reprinted or reproduced or utilised in any form or by any electronic, mechanical, or other means, now known or hereafter invented, including photocopying and recording, or in any information storage or retrieval system, without permission in writing from the publishers.

Trademark notice: Product or corporate names may be trademarks or registered trademarks, and are used only for identification and explanation without intent to infringe.

British Library Cataloguing-in-Publication Data
A catalogue record for this book is available from the British Library

Library of Congress Cataloging-in-Publication Data
Names: Freeman, Kate (Speech therapist), author. | Edge, Jenny, illustrator.
Title: Sleep time : a Words Together storybook to help children find their voices / Kate Freeman ; illustrated by Jenny Edge.
Description: New York, NY : Routledge, 2022. | Series: Words together |
Summary: Illustrations and simple, repetitive text reveal that everyone is sleeping.
Identifiers: LCCN 2021032369 (print) | LCCN 2021032370 (ebook) | ISBN 9781032151885 (pbk) | ISBN 9781003242925 (ebk)
Subjects: CYAC: Sleep—Fiction. | Toddlers—Fiction. | LCGFT: Picture books.
Classification: LCC PZ7.1.F75458 Sl 2022 (print) | LCC PZ7.1.F75458 (ebook) | DDC [E]—dc23
LC record available at https://lccn.loc.gov/2021032369
LC ebook record available at https://lccn.loc.gov/2021032370

ISBN: 978-1-032–15188-5 (pbk)
ISBN: 978-1-003–24292-5 (ebk)

DOI: 10.4324/9781003242925

Typeset in Candy Randy
by codeMantra

Dedicated to Bryony, Arthur, Chay, Harvey and Sandy, alongside all the children I have cared for and worked with. These people, their families and early years settings are the inspiration for the Words Together series of books.

Cat sleeping.

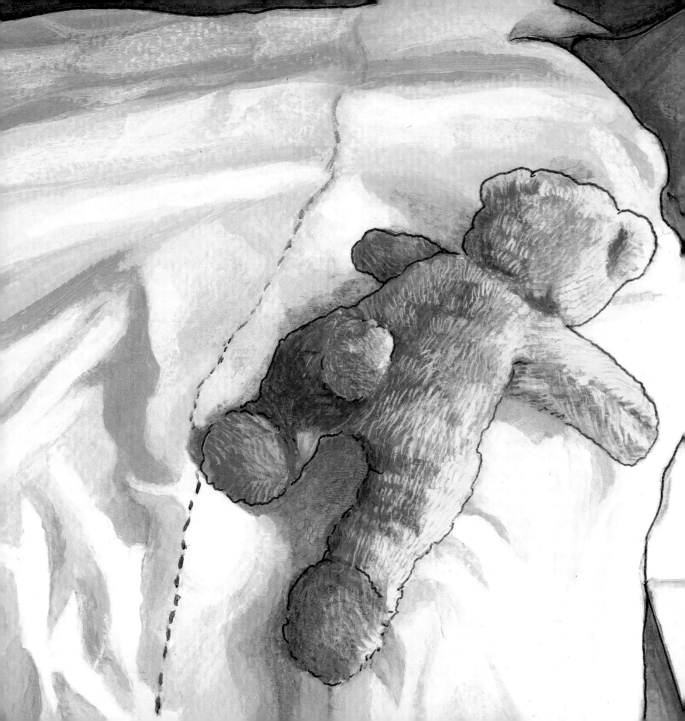

Teddy sleeping.

Monkey sleeping.

Baby sleeping.

Everyone sleeping.